I can move

How I breathe   I can move
I am growing   When I eat

First published in 1991 by
Firefly Books Limited
61 Western Road, Hove
East Sussex BN3 1JD, England

© Copyright 1991 Firefly Books Limited

This edition published in 1993 by Wayland (Publishers) Ltd

Editor: Mandy Suhr
Consultant: Roy Hawkey

British Library Cataloguing in Publication Data
Suhr, Mandy
I can move.–(I'm alive)
I. Title   II. Series
612.7

HARDBACK ISBN 1-85485-130-6

PAPER BACK ISBN 0-7502-0914-3

Typeset by DP Press, Sevenoaks, Kent
Printed in Belgium by Casterman. S.A.

I can move

Written by Mandy Suhr

Illustrated by Mike Gordon

Wayland

When I was born
I was very
little.

I could kick my feet
and move my arms
but I couldn't even
sit up.

I had to be carried everywhere.

As I grew, my bones and muscles got bigger and stronger.

Soon I could move around on my own.

I can move in lots of different
ways now.

I can skip . . .

run . . .

jump . . .

roll and dance.

I can do all these things because
I have a skeleton inside my body.

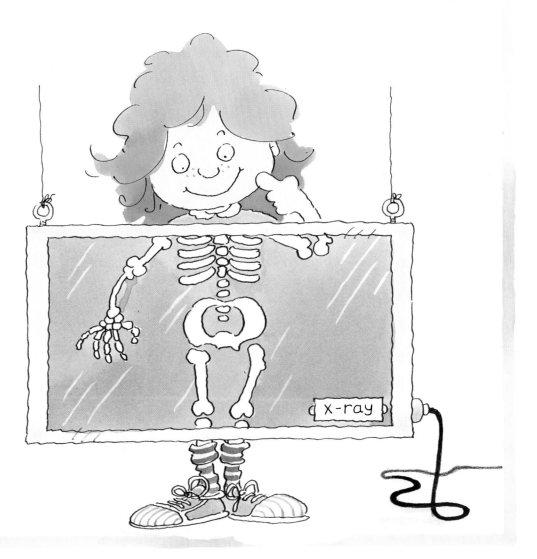

If I didn't have one I wouldn't be able to stand up, I'd be all floppy!

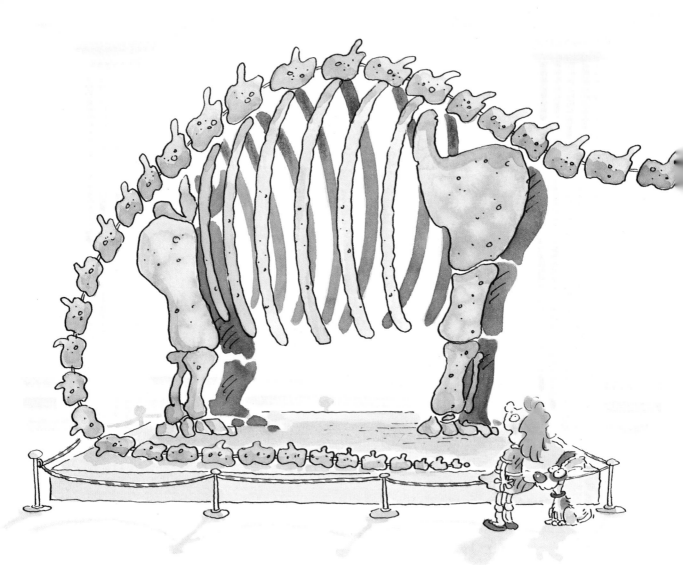

Our skeletons are made up of
lots of different bones. Big bones
and small bones join together.

Bones are very
hard and strong.

It is the joined bits of our skeleton that move.

My knees and
elbows bend
because this is
where two
bones join
together . . .

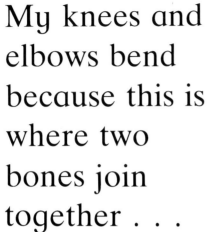

so do my fingers . . .

and my toes.

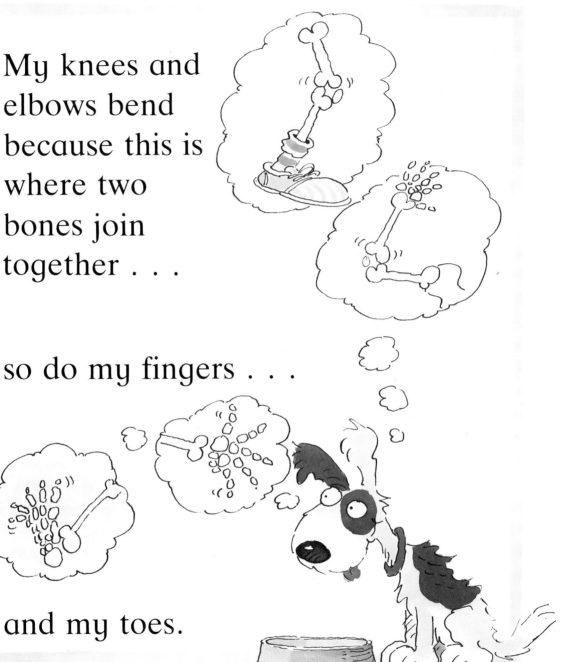

This is my backbone.

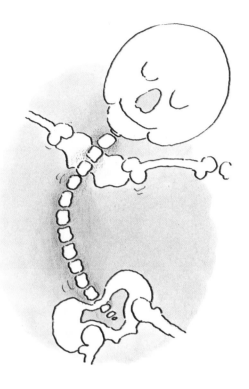

It is really lots of small bones joined together so that it can bend.

It goes all the way from my head down my back to my bottom.

My bones are all moved by
muscles.

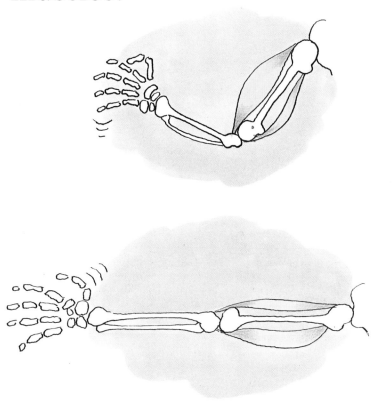

These are like big stretchy elastic
bands joined to the bones.

Muscles pull the bones up and down when I want to move them.

Lots of animals have skeletons like we do.

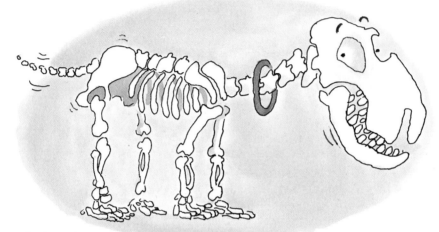

This is my dog Jess.

This is my goldfish Jaws.

Birds have skeletons too.

This skeleton is just like the one inside you or me.

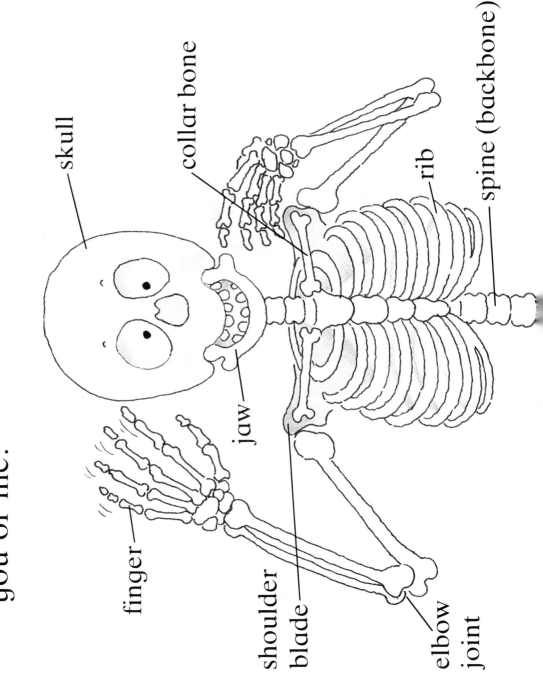

skull

collar bone

rib

spine (backbone)

jaw

finger

shoulder blade

elbow joint

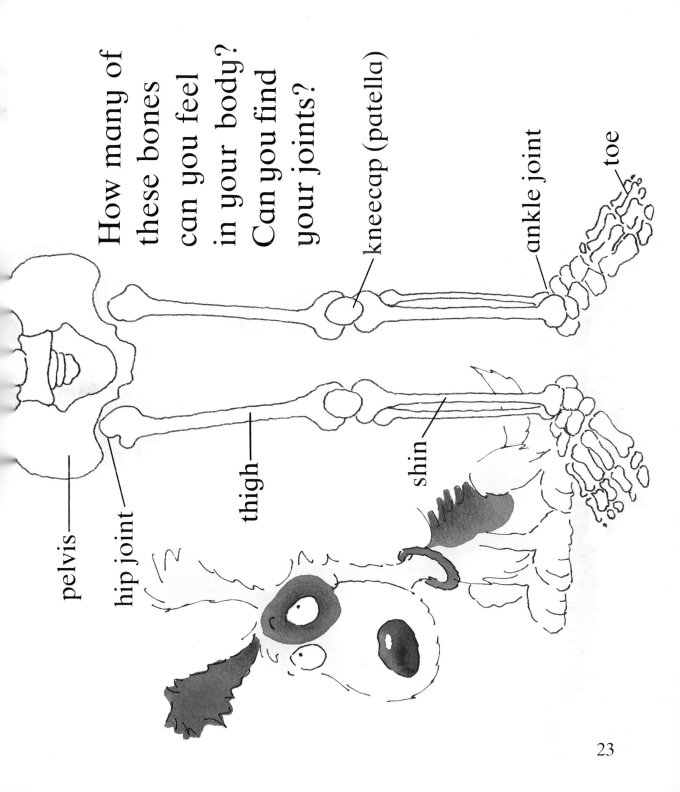

How many of
these bones
can you feel
in your body?
Can you find
your joints?

kneecap (patella)

ankle joint

toe

pelvis

hip joint

thigh

shin

Notes for Adults

'I'm alive' is a series of first information books particularly suitable for the early and emergent stages of reading.

Each book has a simple, factual text, and amusing and colourful illustrations, combining reading for pleasure with fact–finding.

The series takes a closer look at the human body and how it works and develops, comparing this with other forms of life. 'I'm alive' is designed to address the requirements of the National Curriculum for Science keystage 1, Attainment target 3: Processes of life.

The books are equally suitable for use at school or at home. Below are some suggestions for extension activities that can be carried out to complement and extend the learning in this book.

Extension Activities

1 Make a cardboard skeleton. Use brass split pins to join the body parts and locate and make the major joints. Can you count how many different joints there are in your body?

2 Make a poster about the different ways in which you can move your body. Cut out and collect pictures from magazines to stick on to your poster.

3 Move different parts of your body. Feel the muscles getting thinner and fatter as your bones move.

4 Imagine you couldn't move around on your own and had to use a wheelchair or crutches. Find out how easy it would be to get around your home or school.

5 Use mechano and elastic bands to build a model arm.